Introspection

by

Nygie P. Rhodes

DORRANCE PUBLISHING CO
EST. 1920
PITTSBURGH, PENNSYLVANIA 15238

Dorrance Publishing Co
585 Alpha Drive
Suite 103
Pittsburgh, PA 15238
Visit our website at *www.dorrancebookstore.com*

ISBN: 979-8-8872-9422-3
eISBN: 979-8-8872-9922-8

*F*irst, thank you for taking the time out of your day(s) to read this! This means a lot to me. I am an ordinary college student who decided writing on the side was a way to release my thoughts. No matter how wild. You are lucky to read this. I think I have a gift when it comes to articulating myself in a plethora of ways. Or maybe not. You be the judge.

This work is called *Introspection*. I take a deep intellectual look at myself from all angles. My emotions, my mind, my thoughts, my body, etc. Well, at least I think I did. At any rate, thank you again for reading this!!

Author's Note

Some of what you read is not true,
but most of it is my imagination going wild with a hint of truth.

Beware: Vulgar language in some poems.

The Opening
(Read this pretty darn fast)

This is the opening to something, a new beginning
They told me I was peculiar and different than what they expected
They always wonder what goes on in my head and I am always questioned
I always tell them my mind operates different
This is something, a new beginning
A new look at who I am as a human being
I developed an evolved mind, one that expands
and gets more deranged over time
I take a close look in the mirror and try to decode
who I see on the other side
I take a closer look and realize I am being seen
as something else in the mirror's eyes
This is the opening, a new beginning
Trying to understand who I am emotionally and internally
An expanded look at who I am as Nygie
An expanded understanding of each cell that creates me
The God to a universe, a Picasso to his paintings
A singer to their songs, the words to its meaning
A verse in the Bible, the meaning thereof
The Preacher to the choir, and all the above
Trying to understand what we are made of and our meaning
THIS IS THE OPENING, A NEW BEGINNING
Come into my mind and take a trip with me
To unveil the mystery of my work of art
The color of my thoughts
The darkness in my emotions
The light in my expressions
My palpitations in my heart
The race in my mind
The double me I see

WHAT IS THE MIND
Victim mentality
And how murderous I can feel
And many more you'll see if you just come with me
On my journey to a new beginning.

Not The Same

Have you not seen the peculiarness while in the presence of this being?

Why, Mom?
Am I looked at strange
Seen as something not worth talking to
Seen as something not worth questioning
Labeled as "different"
Tattooed as attention
Thought of as this
Never asked why or what
Just told me I was
Not the same
They told me I was not the same.
Observed because I move quickly
Studied because I am there in their presence
Watched because they sit still and I am in motion
Examined due to my character

Why, Mom?
Did you ever not see my distinctive characteristics
It could have been caught sooner and maybe prevented it
I could be the same
I could be understood
Not shamed
Not ashamed of what I am
But it was not my choice
This is who I am
But I am not them
Not the same
They told me I was not the same.

Why, Mom?
Was I made fun of
I stood out so much
I became a laughing joke
A something to point a finger at
A nothing in their eyes
A something to a punching bag
A nothing in humanity
Not thought of as them
I was different
Not alike to them
Not the same
They told me I was not the same.

Why, Mom?
Must they lash out at me
People release their anger, guilt, hate, and insecurities
At me to make them feel free
As I walk in shackles
BUT I AM ALSO HUMAN
I feel just like they do
But people live in a world of just them and no one else
I stay in my world
My world is different
Not alike to their world
I am different
I am
Not the same
They told me I was not the same.
Observed because I move quickly
Studied because I am there in their presence
Watched because they sit still and I am in motion
Examined due to my character

Have you not seen the peculiarness while in the presence of this being?

I Stand

(Continue to read fast)

I am an individual that stands out, who stands proud! I move to the flow of my own symphony.

From a challenge I will not back down

I have learned behind my back I must watch out

For people and their schemes.

I am an individual that's deeply intellectual

My mind thinks on different levels.

It can be hard to understand, but instead of trying to comprehend

You'd rather distend your distance to avoid trying to make amends with what I think.

I can be hard to read, but instead of trying to read every word in the sentence, you just look at the punctuation trying to concoct what you think should be the ending of the sentence missing key words and phrases.

I am an individual that stands out, who stands proud! I am someone that is often questioned.

The infamous why and what, the how and when, but never I respect, I get, I love you, man. I understand I may not be what I should be by your standards or beliefs

I understand my beliefs are in opposition to yours and I try to explain my rationale but you won't listen. Rather you ignore any reasoning and develop a dour expression looking incredulously at me like a mirror reflection.

Two humans with no connection.

I am one who is always left walking

Away from the disturbance of people who interrupt my internal peace and rhythm.

My Internal World

(Read Regularly)
My internal world
Is my home
It's where I can be peaceful, imagine, believe, hope, be free
It's where I can have no care in the world
I am free from a bad society
I can be one with my soul, my intellect

My internal world
Is precious to me
It's where I run to when I need
A time to be away from the reality of the world
It's where I hide
To be myself
It's where I go
When I can't interact with the world

My internal world
Is my everything
When people disrupt my life
My place of solitude reassures me that everything will be okay
Alone I cannot be harmed
Alone I can understand myself and be happy
As some people struggle to understand me

My internal world
Is my love
When love cannot be brought to me by another
Myself must compensate
To prevent the damage of not being wanted
Myself must compensate

To lessen the feeling of confusion
Of why myself, internal, struggles to connect with another
Myself must compensate
My internal world
Whispers to me when no voice speaks to me
To allow my voice to be heard
To give me another entity
To interact with
A connection

My internal world
Is my home
It's where I can be peaceful, imagine, believe, hope, be free
It's where I can have no care in the world
I am free from a bad society
I can be one with my soul, my intellect…

…Myself.

One who…
(Read fast again)
..Stands Proud!
Proudly I stand and proudly I will always walk!
Though there are entities out there who stalk and prey
On me to fall or give in to their unrighteous ways
Righteously I will stride forward passing you as the evil weight you carry
holds you down.
You attempt down to your last breath to grab my hand and drag me down
with you
While you wrongfully, graciously hope that we both drown suffocating to-
gether as your life goes down. You attempt to bring me down like me using
the word down repeatedly while trying to keep a rhythm with someone want-
ing to change my beat and you often do this consistently.

I am also consistent with conducting my own symphony.

If you don't like it get off my stage and join the audience in the seats.

You can applaud later and throw roses at my feet.

As I walk away proudly!

Dreams of Flames and Fire

(From here on out read regularly)

That's pretty bold of you to think that you stand out more than the rest of us, Nygie!

Fuck off. Not every flame has the same heat coming from it. Some flames are meant to burn their subject more. Don't test my flame.

Dreams of fire burning the environment around me
Dreams of flames becoming bigger with gasoline
Gasoline coming from my sudden burst of rage and becoming irritable
Dreams of heat being brought upon them for the pain
Dreams of bright light stemming from a dark intention
Like getting to know you for quick pleasure in the bedroom.

Dreams of the after-effect
The smoke will remind us all that each of us has a fire that can be ignited
I hope people can see the signs and learn how to heed to it
No.
I hope that people can listen when someone speaks from their heart
expressing what they are going through and have faith that their voice will
be enough for people to stop.
No.
People ignite the fire and will run before the heat catches them
Too late.

Dreams of a fire burning to make them understand
Dreams of flames making them squirm
Dreams of people to burn
Dreams of flames and fire

He Races His Mind Endlessly

He races his mind endlessly
Opening up an internal passageway to the trouble that is to be
Causing his body to prepare for a channel of rush
One mite thought to inch the blood forward
His thoughts are the energy that will subdue his body to the submission of
his mind
He races his mind endlessly
Formulating his heart to prepare for overdrive
Preparing his main source to force the blood through the channels
Preparing his body to ache excruciatingly

His body left hopeless
His body left no power
His body tied in chains, his mind has trapped his body
His body fearful
His body crying
His body pleading
To an end of the race

As his mind races his vessels pop
The blood overflowing in his body and overfilling the channels
Generating pain and aching of his body
Producing his body to feel numb
Convincing his body it's not there
His body to feel the sensations of what emotions
are embodied coming from his thoughts

As his mind gets faster his body goes into an uncontrollable internal pulsing
attack, making his body wish it could separate itself from the mind to stray
away from the linkage of pain from the mind that causes its pain, to the mind
that has the body in chains to the mind that is holding the body hostage.

No escape body. Just suffer.
He races his mind endlessly
Opening up an internal passageway to the trouble that is to be
Causing his body to prepare for a channel of rush
One mite thought to inch the blood forward
His thoughts are the energy that will subdue
his body to the submission of his mind
He races his mind endlessly
Formulating his heart to prepare for overdrive
Preparing his main source to force the blood through the channels
Preparing his body to ache excruciatingly

Yourself

Who have you brought before me?

> Yourself. True in its nature, true to its creation.

Why now?

> It's time. If it was not for yesterday, today would not have been had for you to become more aware of yourself.

Why did it slowly progress?

> Don't be foolish. Your mind was too young in the past. Besides, without the environment you were put in none of this would be happening.

Being alone, isolated, alienated, forgotten, not understood, rejected, this is what causes one to become more aware of themselves?

> If no one is in your way all you have to think about is yourself. Think about why you are isolated.

Therefore allowing myself to understand who I am as deep as possible?

> Yes.

Why am I different?

> Why are you not alike?

Why am I not understood?

It's easier to not understand than it is to try.

It's having an effect on me.

What is?

The steps that were construed by whoever controls life forcing me to learn deeply about myself.

Go on.

I feel…like…sudden rages…at times I feel like I am someone else, or something else. I feel like this unknown force creeping upon me into my body. Controlling me…

Anonymously Unintroduced

You crept upon me with silence
Slowly to contrive what is meant to be
It was a matter of time
You are the hands to the clock
Positioning yourself for the right moment
And you chose to strike now
You've hid in the shadows for too long
All the while knowing it was a matter of time before you couldn't prolong
Your existence
You move by the second
Steadily taking control over your corpse
Knowing the interior design of the corpse will be anew
As you have grasp the inside
As you have grip over the pulse
Anonymously unintroduced
You strangle my veins and vessels
You are alike to a Python
Constricting me as I fall under your control
Left nowhere to run, nowhere to go
Deteriorating internally
A leisure pace
You are the trigger to the gun
My heart the bullet
A concatenation of events
When you decide to pull
My heart and blood rushes
Like a pool of blood leaving a body from a fatal stab of a machete
You are the hands that choke my interior
Slowly you position your hands around
Knowing one day you must make your move to end me
You chose to strike now

Anonymously unintroduced
You leave me an empty body
A disturbed pulse
With painful movement
You strike my body convulses
Going into a state of burst
Uncontrollably
You crept upon me with silence
Slowly to contrive what is meant to be
It was a matter of time
You are the hands to the clock
Positioning yourself for the right moment
And you chose to strike now
You've hid in the shadows for too long
All the while knowing it was a matter of time before you couldn't prolong
Your existence

You are one with no moniker
An enigmatic figure
A secret to the silence
Quiet to a whisper
A blind to the darkness
You are a hidden weapon
For self-destruction
From within

Anonymously unintroduced

Double Entity

This entity staring into a mirror
Forced to see the resemblance of himself
Forced to see the framework of a creation
A framework seen on the outside
This entity staring into a mirror
Cannot see the resemblance internally from his own reflection
The mirror fails to reveal the interior design of the framework
It does not mirror the foundation of the core like that of the outside
This entity staring into a mirror
Wonders if his resemblance mirrors his internal pulse
His vehemence, his intensity, his compulsion, his spirit.
If at all, does his resemblance have a conscience
This entity staring into a mirror
Questioning to himself if his resemblance and himself both know
Knowing that if one knows
Then the other must also know
If they resemble one another
This entity staring into a mirror
Wonders if his resemblance has the same fate
One reflection with the will to depart life
The other, the will to depart his bondage from his reflection
This entity staring into a mirror
Inquisitive on the purpose of his resemblance
Does he merely exist only when glanced upon through a glass
This entity staring into a mirror
Forever inquisitive if what he sees is him at all
Forever inquisitive if what he sees is him at all

Another

With due time
Your body is mine

I will walk identical to you
I will speak your voice
I will love with your heart
I will think with your brain
I will

I am another you

I will see with your eyes
I will breathe with you
I will feel your rhythm
I will dance with your body
I will

I'm in you

I will become your pain
I will touch upon your emotion
I will be a deceiver
I will take over
I will

Deep within

I will emerge from the deep to be present from the shallow
You will drown as I arise
Fighting to keep control
I will be the new possessor
You will be an acolyte
This will be...

A switch of an entity
A switch quiet to a whisper
A switch even the seer won't see
A switch no mirror can replicate
I will be swift
I will be deep within...

Yourself

With due time
Your body is mine

My soul will replace yours
My thoughts will acquire your mind
My saunter to change the beat
My pulse will change the rhythm
Myself a new beginning
My eyes to offer a new perception
My sensation to seek affection
My drive to move faster
My voice distinct
My words vitriolic

As you weaken

You will fade
You will fall
You will be lost
You will disappear
You will give in
Into my submission
With due time
Your body is mine

I am another you

The Power of a Million Emotions

The million emotions
Are the tempo to my body's song
Conducting from the inside
My heart its baton
My body the vessel
As the emotions move freely

The power of emotions
Impels my body to dance
To the rhythm of the emotion
Every step, breath, inch of movement
Choreographed by the emotion's hand

The surge of my blood rushing
Will compel my body to move
In ways it has never before
The grip of the emotion leaves my body to endure

The power of emotions
Flows within me like a river
A constant flow not easily disrupted
Not even from a quick switch in its motion
My blood the water
My pulse the current

The million emotions
Are the tempo to my body's song
Conducting from the inside
My heart its baton
My body the vessel

As the emotions move freely

A million emotions I feel a day
With none to keep me sane
The myriad waves of adrenaline
The blood rushing within my veins
A million emotions I feel a day
A million switches in mood and thoughts
Modulating back and forth with my internal intensity
As if my emotions are a swing set
A million switches in mood and thoughts
A switch I cannot turn off
For as long as my brain and my emotions are connected
This internal tragedy will never be lifted

A million unanticipated feelings
Plunge upon me like rain from a storm
A million I can't control
My own feeble sanity to keep me warm
A million beats per minute
A constant wave change in seconds

The power of emotions
Impels my body to dance
To the rhythm of the emotion
Every step, breath, inch of movement
Choreographed by the emotion's hand

Saunter and Sumpter

Saunter

A leisure walk into the grips of others' evil

Trying to pull away from it

To stroll with life as peaceful as one should be

But the disturbance of the evil causes tyranny

To the individual who wants peace

Oppressed by their constant wicked ways

Saunter

Away from what cannot harmonize with tranquility

If a slight interference severs the calamity

The peaceful state is hard to find

Taking time to find stillness can become hard if evil extends the process

Saunter

Away to a place to find freedom

Freedom of pain, hurt, fighting, war, interaction from society

Free to enjoy life as one would hope to be

Free to imagine the realm of unity and solidarity

Saunter

Into a deep internal walk with oneself

Introspection

To find any disturbances to a harmony from oneself

Only to find some of those delays are caused by outside forces

Saunter

To find the answer to why those outside forces halts the harmony

Except the answers are nowhere to be found

Left to wonder how the individual can become at peace

Saunter

Forever to walk

Forever to stroll

Forever moving forward towards peace

Sumpter
Packing their evil onto humans
Placing their wickedness onto others
To carry their evil weight around
Disrupting peace
Sumpter
Intentionally shattering any internal harmony one searches for
Stripping and prolonging the saunter for calamity
With malicious intentions wanting no peace
Sumpter
Projecting their lack of internal understanding of themselves forward onto others
Trying to live vicariously to feel the peace others may have
Is their only way to understand peace

Sumpter
The weight of their problems onto people
Not understanding that issue
Will have an affect
On ones searching for peace
Sumpter

Saunter for peace
Sumpter to halt the peace

My internal world of saunter and sumpter

Swift, cold, calming, sounding.
Wind
Quick, long, light, heavy.
Wind

We cannot see wind, but we feel it.
We walk outside and we know it's there, even when it doesn't blow.

Makes us feel cold, makes us feel cooled off.
Wind
Makes us feel good, makes us cry.
Wind

We cannot perceive the emotions of the wind, nor can we anticipate the strength of the wind. We cannot walk around the wind or lie low and hope the wind misses us.

It comes in big gusts or small gusts.
Wind
Powering through anything in its way.
Wind

We can make wind if it's not present by running, for example. We can force wind upon people, a swing set for example.

Swift, cold, calming, sounding.
Wind
Quick, long, light, heavy.
Wind

We cannot see wind, but we feel it.
We walk outside and we know it's there, even when it doesn't blow.
Evil is the wind.

Stay

Can you stay with us?
Do not leave and make us bleed.
Without your presence we are left to believe
That the world made you leave.
With you gone we are left to question where it started and where it all went wrong. We want to think the world is worth the stay.
At times we agree it can be a brutal place. But you have to forget about the pain.
And stay. Don't go.
Do not leave us in woe.

Can you stay with us?
We can cause you trouble and make you bleed. We can also heal you and make you feel relieved. We are a game of back-and-forth.
Back to pain, and forward to heal.
If you choose to leave that is your fault.
Choosing to not talk or get help is you losing by default.

But people are so irritating and malicious. Sometimes it's too much
to bear. Especially when you
try to talk to people about it but they won't list...

...Excuse me, we were talking. Before I was rudely interrupted.
It's you yourself who gets corrupted. It's you who must change perspectives.
We hear you at times.
Others, you need to stop complaining.

Not quite accurate. Sometimes I can understand the rationale and motive with some people. Sometimes I need to hear and see from your side and give up my view. But the overwhelming weight of being the minority perspective on most...

...Exactly, give yourself up to us. Become one with us.

Some things I should try, but other things;
what you guys do sometimes is brutal.

Either become brutal or be beaten.

Cannot you change to my side?

No.

Hmm. Become brutal or be beaten, you say?... I can be more brutal
than what you think. Be careful what you wish for.

Can you stay with us?
Do not leave and make us bleed.
Without your presence we are left to believe
That the world made you leave.
With you gone we are left to question where it started and where it all went
wrong. We want to think the world is worth the stay.
At times we agree it can be a brutal place. But you have to forget about the pain.
And stay. Don't go.
Do not leave us in woe.

I have no intentions of going.
What's hard is trying to find positive energy.
Finding a sense of understanding.
Finding a sense of righteous morality.
From people. And quite frankly, people are not loyal. People go be-
hind your back and do things recklessly.
It's sickening. And I am SICK of it.
Don't leave and make you bleed, you say.
Hahahahaha
You'll bleed, alright.

Behind My Back

Behind my back I cannot see.

The malicious schemes being contrived to cause casualties relationally. The secrets from the ones who I trusted.

The hidden intentions from them became corrupted.

I must find a way to overcome and stay robust, sometimes it's tough. This isn't a matter of them versus me and me being the victim.

Battles happen in life and this one I must overcome. Me vs. them.

Behind my back I cannot see. The plans to go against me.

I must move forward and allow their scheme to face me. Right then and there I will act to protect.

Right then and there I will wreak havoc.

The sadistic characteristics of the most wicked

Will be the ones who cause the most corrupted commotion. The sadistic characteristics of the most immoral and wrong intend to see a human fall and they smile.

The sadistic characteristics of the most ill

Likely to not empathize for others as they still

Want to ensure damage to the life of another.

Going about their lives as if nothing is happening.

Hidden in the shadows they live, a secret to the silence. A goodwill they will not give, they are a walking menace. Not to be seen by any public eye, they're good.

A light from God will still not show their presence, they are sealed in the shadows for good. A cry that they exist will be ignored, even when the truth is revealed.

A bunch of fucking idiots and don't-want-to-accept-the-truths are what keeps them in existence.

Behind my back I cannot see.

The malicious schemes being contrived to cause casualties relationally.
The secrets from the ones who I trusted.

The hidden intentions from them became corrupted.

I must find a way to overcome and stay robust, sometimes it's tough.
This isn't a matter of them versus me and me being the victim.

Battles happen in life and this one I must overcome. Me vs. them.

Victim Mentality

Change your mind, it becomes not a problem.
Change your thought process and watch the issue go away.
Change everything about your psyche and you're fine.
Change your perception, the problem disintegrates.
I think not.
You are confined in your way of thinking, a false illusion.
What you see is only the outcome of your analysis
What is this?

No matter the environment, it has no effect.
No matter the reality, what you see is false.
No matter the probative evidence, it was concocted.
No matter the veracity of your story, you don't know the truth.
I think not.
You are trapped with how you've perceived the event.
What you see is only an illusion, a fixed reality.
What is this?

Listen to them, not your voice.
Listen to their side, not yours.
Understand their mind, forget yours.
Understand their rationale, you cannot think.
Hear them, never listen to yourself.
Hear them, hear them.
I think not.
You are tasked with being wrong all the time.
What you think you know, you don't.
What is this?

You cannot control how you perceive something the first time, but over time you have the ability to reflect back on that precise moment in which you perceive something, only to change it. Only to change it in your mind.

Because that is what you must do. Change your mind.

Over time you can see the truth in something. However, you must alter the perception over the time of you seeing what you see because what you see is false. Change your mind. Change your mind.

Your mind is a powerful tool. It has abilities far beyond the ordinary understanding. You have immersed yourself into your mind, to see a world more expanded than what you thought you were capable of.

Are you scared?

Are you ready to see the world, a new reality, from an expanded ability to understand people, their motives, the world, evil, good, humans?

Do you like your new eyes, your new wear? Do you like your new mind?

…

Victim mentality.
Nothing is wrong, except the way you think.
Victim cry.
Hide those tears, suppress those emotions.
Victim violin.
No matter how sweet the song, no one will listen. You're wrong.
Victim me.
No, no, no, no one did anything. Stop it.
Victim, hear my voice.
You are silenced forever.
Victim, see my side.
There's only one side, the other side. Stop being a victim. They don't exist.

Victim's mind
No, victim mentality.
I think not.

Something Feels Off

…

Hello, Nygie! What brings you to me?

I feel anger. I feel frustrated. I feel betrayed.

And something feels off.

I can't understand, I can't interact anymore.

I feel misunderstood.

I feel lost.

The mind I carry is esoteric.

Some people fear it.

I'm afraid most people can't comprehend my perspective.

Most say I'm senseless. Something is numb.

Inside me.

Maybe it's my fault and only I can set myself free.

But the question is, who caged me?

Myself, or society? Something feels off.

My heart beats faster than what my circulatory system anticipates.

The sudden palpitations reminds me of a drummer who is off rhythm

Not able to slow his hands to get back on beat or feel the tempo within him.

I walk slowly in the night, hoping my race ends with my heart

and it can rest after running a marathon

But soon I will be gone racing once more knowing my heart will take off.

I feel rejected from the people who I should mostly feel endured by

and last over time

My environment is supposed to show me the light through struggles and

give me hope and faith to see another day

BUT DAMN, I feel like I am so different than the people around me

Forcing me to alienate myself from them if I want to keep my peace

I feel trapped in the sense of I can't interact with them

Or If I decide to connect with them I will end up in chains

Brought to me by them.

Yours truly, your environment.

Have you experienced anything like this before in your past?

No.

What you are experiencing is a culture shock. You are being subjected to a new environment, the real world.

Do you feel disoriented when being in certain situations?

Sometimes.

You are experiencing a different culture than what you're used to. How do you respond to that?

Violence.

That is not the way to handle things, Nygie.

Let me ask you this, what is the difference between someone
who is violent with their slick, conning,
malicious scheming behaviors vs. a physically violent person?

Nygie, you cannot be violent in any way, shape or form. That is not acceptable.

So physical violence is not acceptable?

Nygie!!

I may plan to hurt people emotionally or mentally then.
I'll just pain them under the cover.

THAT IS NOT OKAY!!

> FUCK YOU, BITCH, TELL THAT TO THE PEOPLE THAT
> BROUGHT ME HERE!!!

NYGIE!!

Take This with a Grain of Salt

Take this with a grain of salt.

I know yourself more than you do.

I know your limits and what you are capable of. You do not.

I know what you can accomplish and cannot. I know, I know.

Take this for what you will.

I know how I can make you feel.

I know what goes on inside of you internally. You do not.

I tell you how you feel, how you think. I tell, I tell.

Just take this.

Who I see in my reality is what you are.

Even if you grow or discover new gifts, it's not real. It can't be real if my reality does not allow it to be. Your reality does not matter.

Mine does. Mine does.

Accept it.

Whatever I say goes. My words speak for you. You have no voice.

You can't have one.

My voice has to be heard. My voice, my voice.

I am right.

My thoughts and beliefs are what yours are. My mind is your mind, you cannot be different. You and I must think the same.

You cannot think differently. My mind, my mind.

> Doesn't this work both ways? If you, a human being, can take on this
> type of mentality of squeezing everyone to fit your
> reality, whose reality are you truly in?
> Yours or another human's?

Amorality

Indifference to the code of society.

Indifference to the standards of what should be. No care for what damage to life.

No care for the severed peace. No responsibility for your actions.

No responsibility to want to understand them. No sight for righteousness.

No sight for good.

Evil you want to prevail. Evil you entail.

You don't know who you are internally. You struggle to find yourself.

You don't know what you believe in. You don't know your values.

You do not care.

Indifference to the rules of life. Indifference to the boundaries of another.

No care for solidarity.

No care for togetherness. No responsibility to love.

No responsibility for the man above. No sight for anyone.

You selfish bastard. Evil you all are.

Evil you wield.

Indifference to the code of society.

Indifference to the standards of what should be. No care for what damage to life.

No care for the severed peace.

You.

Amorality.

You.

Dead.

Murder

Destruction on my mind
To kill, to harm, to hurt. Relieve me, free me.

Take me away to rot with Satan, to burn.
In the flames I will be. My hands with blood on them from murder-
ing.
Throw me with the demons
Those vicious beasts.
As the pain of living this life is enough.

When you want to take away a life they remind you of the worth of one. When you want to leave this world they remind you the world is good. As you stay living life you have to suffer at the hands of evil. As you stay living life you have to suffer at the hands of people. As you stay present in the world, you must not leave, That's ungrateful. Ungrateful to the memories you've built. Ungrateful to the future that awaits you. Ungrateful to the world built to you from corrupted and flawed beings. Ungrateful for removing yourself from society. Ungrateful for not allowing more fucked- up people to wrong you. How dare I?

How selfish can you be?
Selfish for thinking about you and not me.
Selfish for thinking about your pain and not my suffering.
Selfish of you to see the evil and not the good even though you tried but evil was stronger. Selfish for you to speak out against evil not wanting us to win. Selfish of you to say how you feel and think and think people will try to make a difference. Selfish of you to think about yourself and not families.
You selfish bastard.

It's time for revenge. Destruction on my mind
To kill, to harm, to hurt. Relieve me, free me.

Murder, Murder, I am to die anyway
What's the deal to kill before I am done?
Pain is the deal. I am to live again. Either in hell or heaven. I can be for-
given?

I can. I can quietly pray and hope to not harm.
I prayed for a better life and a second chance.
No answers or responses. I won't ask questions, just harm.
I am to die anyway. What's the deal for the thrill to kill?
Suffering and constant recklessness from human beings.
You can be reckless too, just by killing.
I can be forgiven?

I tried to tell them to back off, I was getting heated. They listened to my
warning and chose not to heed to it.
I tried to articulate it. They did not want to comprehend what was said.
Fuck them, they deserve killing.

Take me away to rot with Satan, to burn.
In the flames I will be. My hands with blood on them from murdering.
Throw me with the demons
Those vicious beasts.
As the pain of living this life is enough.

Selfish of you to act back in such a negative way. Fuck you.
Fuck you.
You weak-ass bitch.
You confident-ass fucker.
I am trying to test you and ruin your confidence. Let me, bitch.
You dare to question me and respond back to me.

You selfish bastard.

You ungrateful-ass human being.

I have my problems but I love the feel of the thrill I get from treating people like a toy. Do you want to play?

NO!

Fuck you.

Destruction on my mind
To kill, to harm, to hurt. Relieve me, free me.

You need to stop. I won't stop with my bullshit, but you need to stop.

THAT'S NOT FAIR!!!

I showed you the signs of my slow rage.

Fuck you.

I get to go to heaven even though I fucked some people up on this earth
But you will go to hell for murdering me.
I win.

As do I.

Murder, Murder, I am to die anyway
What's the deal to kill before I am done?
Pain is the deal. I am to live again. Either in hell or heaven. I can be for-
given?

Bastards

Here's to you, steadier, stronger, and better every day. As I grow up memories are made along the way. It breaks my heart that I am sitting here writing this today. Looking back, nothing seemed like anything could stand in my way. And it won't, I will prove that every day.

You will not bring me down into the hell of your life. I will not fall victim to the fire that burns inside of your soul.

Your misery will not include me. Goodbye to you, and your lack of loyalty. You suffer from your greedy needs of pleasure, gratification, and verification. At the price of that you will suffer for not being able to resist temptation.

You are submissive to temptation, you will always fail. You are weak at staying strong and doing what's right.

Your strength is being able to lie. Being able to go behind backs. And wreak havoc.

You weak son of a bitch, I will not have it.

I will not see...

...you ever being loyal to me. Goodbye to you, and your nonexistent loyalty.

The devil has got you every day. You are not strong enough to escape. The devil wants you in hell all the time

And you will constantly suffer for your duplicitous, conning, human crimes.

You are a con, a person who lies. For your lack of goodness, you shall never see the bright side.

Of life. You will always suffer,

The devil has got your tongue. You cannot find any words to tell the truth.

The lies you speak. Goodbye to you, and your lack of loyalty.

Here's to you, steadier, stronger, and better every day. As I grow up memories are made along the way. It breaks my heart that I am sitting here writing this today. Looking back, nothing seemed like anything could stand in my way. And it won't, I will prove that every day.

Square One- I

It appears I am back to square one. Looking again at that mirror trying to discover what is on the other side. Is it my reflection or something else? Sometimes it's hard to tell. I like to think that me and my reflection are the same even though we both have different realities. One of us is not able to escape the pain and suffering we can feel from day to day. The other stuck watching and wondering. We don't even speak words to one another, just silently communicate and somehow we understand each other. One of us thinks we are a little truculent when times call for it, but the other knows he must not lash out. If one of us chooses to lash out, one of us will break the mirror severing our relationship. We enjoy the relationship because us together is our only way to feel and experience companionship, one of loyalty. One of loyalty. No matter what, my reflection and I are always loyal to one another. No matter how terrible each of our own lives ought to be. We know we can trust one another. If I look behind my back, he will also look behind his, but none of us will catch each other staring at our backs with a knife. We both know that there are good people out there like us. Possibly even weird or peculiar like us. We just have to search harder to find them. We must maintain and hold on to our hope and faith. We must believe. We must believe.

Okay (The Inside of Me)

The inside of me will shake and feel weak at times
I will always remind myself I am okay
The inside of me can tremble like a volcano
It does not mean I have to erupt
I do not have to fall victim to the earthquakes of other people
I will walk away and be peaceful
The inside of me does not have to squeeze itself like a python killing its prey
I can grow stronger in my faith and pray for better days
Even if I have to wait
I do not have to allow my rhythm to speed off or change its tempo
I have to remember I am the conductor to my symphony
I am in control
I do not have to allow other people's weight
or issues pressure me into helping them
I will have to walk away and know they got themselves
I have to remind myself there is good as much as there is evil,
I just have to listen to God and find it
I do not have to obey to people who do not care
I do not have to adhere to the ones who are no good for my health
I do not have to
I do not have to
I am free

I know my mind can think some crazy things
No matter what
I am free

Square One-II

The anger has lifted. The pain, confusion, disappointment, all gone. He is fed up with the constant behind-the-back schemes of people, but he has learned to move forward and let go. Life is giving him good to help balance the bad. This is a transition. A good one. One he can rejoice from. It appears he will not look back and try to find answers anymore. Instead, he will look forward and into the good that awaits him. He is not insane, he is not crazy or weird. Ultimately, he is not the same. In a good way. He is not duplicitous or slick to get away with doing something behind people's backs. He does not let people control him or try to stop him from moving forward in life. He realizes that life is a great thing despite the unusual circumstances life brings him. He wakes up with a smile on his face ready to do something great with the day. He looks forward to his future. Whatever that entails. He is loyal, kind, loving, open-hearted, helpful, caring, and above all, he is Nygie.

What Is the Mind

What is the mind if we do not push it to its full limit?
A waste of a gift.
What is creativity if we do not use it to acquire what we want?
A waste of a tool.
What is uniqueness if we do not expose that quality some of us contain?
You become one of them.
What is imagination if we do not imagine extremely?
A waste of a mindful adventure.
What is extending thought if we do not think deeply?
You will stay in the shallow.
What is intellectuality if we do not understand reasoning or a soul?
Nonexistent.
What is intelligence to what is dumb? A measurement of pure nothingness.
What is high-level thinking if you do not know what level is next?
Plain thinking.
What is the mind if we do not push it to its full limit?

The End

**The next couple of poems are just extras.
They do not pertain to the story.**

She

She

Is the one any man would dream for.

She is the one that will make you kneel before her

Not on one knee, saying, "Will you marry me?"

Instead saying, "How can I please you more?"

She is the one any man would kill other men for just to feel her sensation, her affection, her love, her body.

She will turn you vicious to fight for her

And as you fight for her, she watches carefully to see how you fight

If you fight weakly, you will die.

At the hands of her duplicitous smile.

Behind that smile she is saying, "I am treating you as a puppet but we both love it." Her love is hard to get because she really can be hard to understand but that's okay.

If it's worth trying to get her love she will make a man bend over backwards for her to make her say "I love you" in any way.

It's just that the words are hard for her to find. Even harder for a man to get her to search for it.

At times she makes a man feel like he is not wanted. By shifting her focus elsewhere as you wonder

Why.

At times she makes you feel challenged as she can hold her own and boldly show her intelligence while liking competition.

Are you strong enough to compete?

At times she makes a man want to hold her because she is upset, but she declines making that feeling erect. Become stronger.

How much longer can you hold that in?

She can make you feel like you better do what she says or risk losing her or even a chance at her love, as you tremble on the inside increasing your nerves.

She can flash a light of confusion
As there is more to her that's hidden.
She makes you run your mind at great lengths to try to rationalize what is
underneath the cover, but she is good at sleeping under the sheets forever
making you wonder.

Why you go for her.

She is pretty. I would love to feel her affection. I would love to feel the sensa-
tion of love as we decide that we want our lives interlaced. I would never let
her go. I love being
around her, she makes me smile. For moments on end. Sometimes I choke
and I am at a loss of words. I cannot say anything coherent or show that I
love her. Sometimes I'm scared. That I may make the wrong move and end
it all right there. Jeopardize myself or the moment.

She is smart. She knows what she wants and she gets it. She knows how to
plan and make things happen. She knows she can outsmart and at times be
cunning. She can make your head spin as she goes about her life running for-
ward, forcing you to speed up to catch her.
Or try to…
To get her love because she's pretty. And you love her.
She knows she is beautiful to where she can get God to make her an Angel
Be the leader of them all as the rest follow.
She knows she can have anyone satisfy her by simply saying, "Come here,
baby."
It's just that those same words are the ones used to play you.
She knows she is sweet like a baby clinging on to her mother smiling
As her taste makes you not want to leave so you stay hoping.
To get her love.
She knows you want her love so she makes you try. Over and over again.
Even if you feel like you've failed. You still hope that a boat can set sail. As

the wind guides you.
Hoping that same wind doesn't destroy you.

She knows she can tempt you like the devil
Make you dance to what she says like a you're a stripper.
She knows she can bring you hell and make you feel pain by her fire
All the while saying you still want her.
You sacrifice your heaven to love her. You sacrifice you to love her.
Hopefully forever.

She
Is the one any man would dream for.
She is the one that will make you kneel before her
On one knee, saying, "Will you marry me?"
"How can I please you more?"
She is the one any man would kill other men for just to feel her sensation,
her affection, her love, her body.
She will turn you vicious to fight for her
And as you fight for her, she watches carefully to see how you fight
Seeing if you're strong enough to hold her heart.
Behind that smile she is saying, "I love you."
Her love is hard to get because she really can be hard to understand but that's
okay.
If it's worth trying to get her love she will make a man bend over backwards
for her to make her say "I love you" in any way.
It's just that the words are hard for her find. Even harder for a man to get
her to search for it.

Loving this woman makes me confused. As this poem might have been. Two
back-and-forth moods of "I love her" and "She is a bitch."

Words Unspoken

(Misleading Actions, Purposely or Not Purposely)

You once told me you loved me and I was hesitant to say those words back. You said you loved me again, and this time, questioned me as to why I did not exchange those words back. Why did you urge me to say those words back? Was it because you wanted from my mouth and heart to say "I love you" to you? Did it mean more than just two "friends"? Or did you want me to speak those words to satisfy you? Why the long hugs? Why tell me about your past abusive relationships? Why tell me at all? Why did you choose me? Why always ask me if I was upset at you randomly throughout the day? Why?

My heart left unsettled from confusion and pain
My dreams filled with you in them to recreate the days
Those dreams became nightmares that deepens the hole in my heart
Questions that reappear but I have no answers to them
Only you have them
And can bring my soul at ease
I am left with no peace

My heart left to carry the burden of dissatisfaction
Accepting I was misled by your actions
Convinced maybe you loved me
Maybe I was blinded by being naive
Convinced we could be
The truth revealed and you tricked me

My mind left wondering
Will I ever know the true meaning
Of your actions towards me
My mind left to wonder
If we would have ever

…

I was confused by your actions
Didn't know if I was being played
At times it seemed like a game
I was lost
I couldn't find your motive
So I kept silent
Forever wishing I hadn't

...

There were words I never spoke to you. Ones that would have communicated I once had feelings for you. To this day I wonder if that would have changed how we interacted with one another. Instead, there was this hidden voice between us that never spoke words. Our actions sometimes spoke words for the voice that was too weak to speak.

My heart stopped beating
After we parted ways I had hoped maybe
To see you again and this time explain it
That I had loved you and I meant it
I had dreamt of becoming one from two
It pains me I kept this from you

My mind on replay
From the beginning to the departure
Except we leave loving each other
Repeating the story with affection
Opening myself up a little more with expression
To tell you my confessions
That I once loved you and I had feelings
The true reason why I brought you gifts upon your graduation
The true reason why I enjoyed hugging you for long sessions
I should have said words but I left them unspoken
My mind on replay

There was this hidden voice between us that never spoke
Actions in place of the unspoken
It just caused confusion
Never arriving at a conclusion
I said nothing when I could have
Now I am left wondering and thinking
If I could have ever altered the ending

There were words I never spoke to you. Ones that would have communicated I once had feelings for you. To this day I wonder if that would have changed how we interacted with one another. Instead, there was this hidden voice between us that never spoke words. Our actions sometimes spoke words for the voice that was too weak to speak.

Except my actions never showed and yours was misleading.

A Dream's Escape

A dream's escape is a dream we all dream. A dream to become a living reality to please us, to fulfill our fantasies. We dream continuously, even when we think we are asleep, we are never asleep. We dream. We wake up to dream about what will happen today, will anything special happen to us that day, will bad news come your way that day. We dream about what is to come. Will we, will I, will us, will this, will that, is it, is that, is this. A dream we all dream.

A sound we all hear. Silence. We want to speak, but how quickly we all shy away from our voices. We know the outside will cover their ears or turn away, but the same ones who will turn away had once wanted to speak, but they are aware of the outside's covered ears. So, they shy away, knowing they once turned their own ears away from someone else's voice. Oh, the sweet unrequited love of the people. The shattered dreams. A dream we all want to escape.

The thoughts we all think, but we condemn anyone who uses words to portray the thoughts, the dreams, we all think. The love, the stress, the success, the what if, the will we, are we, will I, will us, the both of us, look at him, look at her, see them, see they, see that, unique, no the same, no different, not the same, no, yes, maybe, some, all. One voice decides to break free to speak what we all dream, they are trying to take a dream and escape that dream, but the dreamcatchers want that dream also, not to be had, not to escape, for it is a terrible dream. If this dream is freed. Oh, the thoughts we all think, but condemn the ones who tries to bring that thought to light. What about the dream?

A dream's escape is a dream we all dream. A dream to become a living reality, but why must we diminish the reality of the dream? If we know we have dreamt it, why not live it? Why must we surround the dream with walls barricaded with guns and pull the trigger when that dream gets a taste of reality? If you had that dream and wanted it lived, would you not also want someone else to live that same dream?

Why speak when you know you do not listen when someone else speaks? Why attempt to listen when you know you do not want to understand? Are you attempting to speak again? See how this goes full circle?

They dream like you. It's interesting how you both, though, do not want any action partaking in that dream's dream to become reality. You sit on a swing hoping to get pushed from behind making you feel like you're flying, but when you have to push someone, you kneel, not wanting them to feel free.

A dream's escape is a dream we all dream. A dream to become a living reality to please us, to fulfill our fantasies. We dream continuously, even when we think we are asleep, we are never asleep. We dream. We wake up to dream about what will happen today, will anything special happen to us that day, will bad news come your way that day. We dream about what is to come. Will we, will I, will us, will this, will that, is it, is that, is this. A dream we all dream.

Through the Voices around You

Through the voices around you, you understand. Your purpose, your reason. The voices from people can move you like God coming into your presence to save you. The distinct sound from someone can bring chills down your body like the pinnacle of a scene in a horror movie. The energy they give off is something unexplainable. The way it moves your soul, it brings out a unique part of yourself that only the outside voice can bring forth. You sit and wonder when the next voice will show that hidden side of you again. Through the voices around you, you can be heard. The voices in your head are overpowered by the logic and reasonings of others. Their voice to help assist in the flaws of our own voices. Alone your voice can damage you, but together our voices will be uplifting. Today we can be uplifted. Thanks to their voices. Through the voices around you, you are welcomed. You are honored, adored, helped, love is reciprocated not unrequited, you can relax without being on edge, live life happily and fun. Like life should be. Enjoying all the waves of emotions and moments like a sea moving freely.

Through the eyes around you, your vision is expanded. You see outside of yourself. You see the perspectives of other people's emotions, gifts, talents, reasoning, wisdom. You learn how to listen and adapt their teachings to bring out a better version of yourself. Through the eyes around you, you learn how to defend their perspective because you now realize you were the one in the bubble this whole time. They were flying free in the sky learning new ways to improve themselves for better success in life as you walk on the ground now understanding what it takes to fly. You start to develop this sense of fellowship, this sense of just simply asking for advice and watch it be granted. All it takes is for you to want to understand the eyes of them. Not be blinded by your own vision. Through the eyes of others, we can accomplish the issue of what we both see. Our visions united will help us defeat any issue through all avenues of what we envision.

Through their position in life, you learn the essence of time. Where they stand currently, you have the ability to reverse time and reflect back to when you were standing where they are. You reach back in your life's timeline to draw forth a memory or lesson to help them move forward like someone else's reversed timeline assisted you. You look ahead and hope a timeline you try to create will be fulfilled. Like partaking in a relationship, raising a family, being what you want to be. Just make sure to see through the eyes of other people and listen to their voices along the way. Through their position in life, you learn the essence of time. You learn everything I said goes full circle. You will see what you once did not see. You will understand what you once couldn't comprehend. This timeline of life.

We will always reflect and move ahead. We should grow everytime we do this. Can we please make sure we assist people along the way.

www.ingramcontent.com/pod-product-compliance
Lightning Source LLC
Chambersburg PA
CBHW051334150726
47997CB00004B/1456